Investigate Science

A Parade of Plants

by Melissa Stewart

Content Adviser: Jan Jenner, Ph.D.

Reading Adviser: Rosemary G. Palmer, Ph.D.,
Department of Literacy, College of Education,
Boise State University

COMPASS POINT BOOKS ✦ MINNEAPOLIS, MINNESOTA

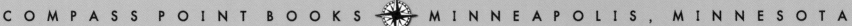

Compass Point Books
3109 West 50th St., #115
Minneapolis, MN 55410

Visit Compass Point Books on the Internet at *www.compasspointbooks.com* or e-mail your request to *custserv@compasspointbooks.com*

Photographs ©: Gregg Andersen, cover (middle), 10, 11, 12, 13 (all), 14, 17, 19, 24, 25; PhotoDisc, cover (background), 1, 9 (bottom right); Digital Stock, 4; Corbis, 5, 6; Eric Crichton/Corbis, 7; Doug Wilson/Corbis, 8; Robert McCaw, 9 (left); Index Stock Imagery, 9 (top right); David Liebman, 15, 16; Dembinsky Photo Associates, 18; Stephen McDaniel, 20; Rob & Ann Simpson, 21; DigitalVision, 22, 23.

Editor: Christianne C. Jones
Photo Researcher: Svetlana Zhurkina
Designer: The Design Lab
Illustrator: Jeffrey Scherer

Library of Congress Cataloging-in-Publication Data
Stewart, Melissa.
A parade of plants / by Melissa Stewart.
    p. cm. — (Investigate science)
Summary: Introduces the parts of a plant, life cycles, and how they grow.
ISBN 0-7565-0592-5 (hardcover)
1. Plants—Juvenile literature. [1. Plants.] I. Title. II. Series.
QK49.S7475 2004
580—dc22   2003018841

Nov 04
5

Note to Readers: To learn about plants, scientists observe them closely. Then they draw and write about everything they see. Later, they use their drawings and notes to help them remember exactly what they saw.

This book will help you study plants like a scientist. To get started, you will need to get a notebook and a pencil.

In the Doing More section in the back of the book, you will find step-by-step instructions for more fun science experiments and activities.

In this book, words that are defined in the glossary are in **bold** the first time they appear in the text.

Table of Contents

As you read this book, be on the lookout for these special symbols:

Read directions *very carefully*.

Ask an adult for help.

Turn to the Doing More section in the back of the book.

Many different
kinds of plants
can grow in
one area.

4

What Is a Plant?

Go outside and look around. How many plants can you spot? Grass is a plant. Trees are plants, too. Many other kinds of plants grow in gardens. Even weeds are plants!

Choose a small plant, and **observe** it carefully. How many leaves grow on each stem? Does the plant grow in the shade or in the sun? Measure the plant's height with a ruler. How tall is it?

If the plant has **flowers,** look at them carefully. What color are they? How do they smell? Draw a picture of everything you see.

Compare your small plant to a tree. How are they similar? How are they different?

Most plants have three main parts—leaves, stems, and 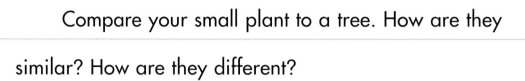 roots. With an adult's help, you can dig up a small plant to find all these parts. Draw the different parts you see.

Most plants have flowers during part of the year. After a flower dies, **fruit** usually appears. Choose a few plants in your yard or a local park. Watch them until you see their flowers and fruits. Draw pictures of what you see. Remember, scientists keep records of everything they observe.

Observe the leaves, stems, and roots of several plants that have flowers.

In the fall, leaves drop off many trees. Collect some of these fallen leaves and sort them by shape, size, and color. Is there any connection between the shape of a leaf and its color? Now look for trees that have not lost their leaves. Watch the trees closely like a scientist would. You will have to watch the trees over many days to see results. Do any of the leaves fall from these trees? Name three ways the leaves of those trees are different from leaves that have fallen off.

Compare the leaves that are still on a tree to the ones that have fallen off.

Trees with different kinds of leaves and colors often grow together.

Living and Growing

Look at some dried beans and some pebbles.
Name three things they have in common. Beans
and pebbles look similar on the outside, but their
insides are very different.

Soak a few beans and pebbles overnight.
How have they changed by morning? Ask an
adult to help you split open one of the beans.
Look at each half closely with a **hand lens.**
Do you see a tiny **sprout?**

A bean is alive. It was made by a
plant and can grow into a new plant. A pebble is not a
living thing. It broke off a larger rock, but it can't grow.
It can only break down more and become sand.

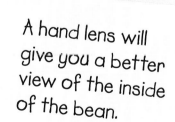

A hand lens will give you a better view of the inside of the bean.

A bean is a **seed.** To see beans grow into plants, you will need some beans, six clear plastic cups, and soil.

Fill the six cups with **soil.** Use one finger to push a bean into the soil in each cup. Be sure to plant each bean along the edge of the cup so you can watch it grow. Add a little water to each cup. Be sure to keep the soil moist, but don't soak it.

How long does it take for the seeds to sprout? Do you see **shoots** or roots first? How long does it take for the first shoot to break through the soil? Draw pictures of the changes you see.

Be sure to have all your supplies ready before you start planting your beans.

Use your finger to push the seed into the soil.

In a few days, you will be able to see the roots, stem, and leaves of the beans you planted.

A kitchen cabinet is a good dark place to put three of your bean cups.

What do plants need to keep growing? To find out, place three of your bean cups in a dark place. Put the other three cups near a sunny window. Check the plants every two days to make sure the soil stays moist. How have the plants changed after a week?

Move all six cups to the place where the plants grow best. Stop watering one of the healthy plants. Spread **petroleum jelly** over the top and bottom of one leaf from a different healthy plant. This will block air from entering tiny holes on the surface of the leaf.

Draw pictures of the plants after a week. What changes do you see? **Predict** what would happen if you covered all the leaves of a plant with petroleum jelly. Write down three things plants need to grow.

Be sure the petroleum jelly covers the top and bottom of the leaf. Record the changes you see after a week.

Lay down paper towels, and place the cup with the third healthy plant on its side. What changes do you see after a few days? Scientists draw pictures to record the changes they observe. You should also draw pictures of what you observe.

Carefully roll the cup onto its other side. What changes do you notice after a few days? Draw another picture to show what happened. What have you learned about how plants grow?

Did You Know?

If the weather is warm, you can replant your healthy bean plants outside in a sunny spot. If you water them, they will flower and produce fruit in about two months.

You can see a dandelion in three different stages all in one place!

Go outside, and find a dandelion plant with a closed bud. Measure the plant's height with a ruler. For the next week, notice the changes in the dandelion. Measure its height each day. How fast does it grow? How long does it take for the bud to open? How long does the flower head last? Do any insects visit it? What happens after the flower head dies? Draw pictures of the changes you see. Can you find the dandelion seeds?

Did You Know?

Dandelion flowers close when it's cloudy and reopen when it's sunny.

Animals Need Plants

An ant can look very different when you examine it through a hand lens!

Look closely at the trunk of a tree. Use a hand lens to get a closer view. Observe the tree's branches and leaves. Look at other plants, too. Do you see any insects? What are they doing? Do you see any other animals on or near the plants in your yard?

Animals could not live without plants. Some animals make their homes in, among, or under plants. Many other animals eat plant leaves, stems, flowers, and fruits.

You can use a small or big hand lens to get a closer look at the creatures crawling on a tree or other plants.

The ingredients in your peanut butter and jelly sandwich come from plants.

Fruits and vegetables come from plants. Plants are also used to make bread, pasta, peanut butter, and chocolate chip cookies. In fact, all the foods you eat come from plants or animals that eat plants!

Take a look around your kitchen. How many foods can you find that are made from plants? Keep hunting until you spot at least 10. Make a list of these foods. Did you eat any of these foods today?

Ask an adult to help you cut an apple in half. Count the seeds inside. Plants make a lot of seeds, but only a few grow into healthy new plants. Make a list of some of the reasons an apple seed might not develop into a new tree.

Now that you've spent some time growing and observing plants, you have a better understanding of their place in our world. Continue to study the parade of plants that grow near your home.

Doing More

Activity One

On page 8 you collected and sorted some fall leaves. Be sure to identify and label each leaf. To keep your collection organized, you can make a plant scrapbook.

1. Place the leaves between two paper towels. Then stack some heavy books on top of the leaves.

2. After a few weeks, take the books off the leaves. Glue each leaf onto a sheet of heavy, white paper.

 3. Ask an adult to help you use a three-hole punch to make holes in each sheet. You can string a piece of yarn through the holes to hold all the pages together.

4. Have an adult help you identify each leaf. Write the name of the leaf on the page. Now you have a leaf scrapbook!

Activity Two

On page 12 you planted some beans and watched them grow. To learn more about how roots grow, try this experiment.

1. Ask an adult to cut the tops off two plastic soda bottles, and punch holes in the bottoms. Place each bottle on a saucer.

2. Fill each bottle halfway with sand. Add 4 inches (10 centimeters) of soil to one bottle and 2 inches (5 centimeters) of soil to the other.

3. Move the bottles to a sunny window. Plant four beans along the edge of each bottle.

4. As the plants grow, watch the roots in each bottle. What differences do you see? Predict what will happen to the roots as the plants continue to grow.

27

Activity Three

On page 20 you learned that many animals depend on plants for food and homes. Plants also make oxygen. People and other animals could not live without oxygen. Oxygen is an invisible gas, but you can see it if you try this experiment.

1. Fill a large, clear bowl with water. Put it in a sunny spot.

2. Slip a small plastic container sideways into the bowl. Let it fill with water.

 3. Carefully flip the container upside down, and place it on the bottom of the bowl. Make sure no air gets into the container.

4. Lift the container just enough to add a few water plants. You can buy water plants at any store that sells fish.

5. Check the container every hour. Draw any changes you see.

6. After a few hours, you should see bubbles rising to the top. They are oxygen bubbles made by the plants. Keep watching the container. What happens next?

Glossary

flower the part of some plants that contains the structures that make new seeds

fruit the part of some plants that surrounds the seed

hand lens a tool that makes objects look bigger than they really are; sometimes called a magnifying glass

observe to use all five senses to gather information about the world

petroleum jelly a thick material that locks in moisture and blocks out air

predict to guess what will happen

seed a small structure that has everything needed to develop into a new plant

shoot the leaf, bud, or new growth on a plant

soil a mixture of broken-up rock and bits of dead plants and animals

sprout a young shoot

To Find Out More

At the Library

Jacobs, Marian B. *Why Do Leaves Change Colors?* New York: PowerKids Press, 1999.

Mitchell, Melanie S. *Seeds.* Minneapolis: Lerner Publications, 2004.

Sprace, Carolyn. *Growing Things.* New York: Franklin Watts, 2002.

Stewart, Melissa. *Plants.* Minneapolis: Compass Point Books, 2003.

Places to Visit

United States Botanic Garden

245 First St. S.W.

Washington, DC 20024

To visit the botanical garden that displays more than 26,000 kinds of plants from around the world

On the Web

For more information on plants, use FactHound to track down Web sites related to this book.

1. Go to *www.compasspointbooks.com/facthound*

2. Type in this book ID: 0756505925

3. Click on the *Fetch It* button.

Your trusty FactHound will fetch the best Web sites for you!

Index

About the Author

Melissa Stewart earned a bachelor's degree in biology from Union College and a master's degree in science and environmental journalism from New York University. After editing children's science books for nearly a decade, she decided to become a full-time writer. She has written more than 50 science books for children and contributed articles to ChemMatters, Instructor, MATH, National Geographic World, Natural New England, Odyssey, Science World, and Wild Outdoor World. She also teaches writing workshops and develops hands-on science programs for schools near her home in Northborough, Massachusetts.